DAVID

Nicholson 1926

DAVID
OF CAMBRIDGE

Some Appreciations

CAMBRIDGE
AT THE UNIVERSITY PRESS
1937

CAMBRIDGE
UNIVERSITY PRESS

University Printing House, Cambridge CB2 8BS, United Kingdom

Cambridge University Press is part of the University of Cambridge.

It furthers the University's mission by disseminating knowledge in the pursuit of
education, learning and research at the highest international levels of excellence.

www.cambridge.org
Information on this title: www.cambridge.org/9781107495043

© Cambridge University Press 1937

First published 1937
First paperback edition 2015

A catalogue record for this publication is available from the British Library

ISBN 978-1-107-49504-3 Paperback

PUBLISHERS' NOTE

THE following tributes need little introduction. All but one of them appeared in the public press within a few days of the news of David's death, and when the suggestion came that they should be printed together, so that David's many friends might have a picture and a memory of him, it was felt that the book would most fittingly bear the Cambridge imprint. Not a few of the rarer books printed by the early University Printers and now in the Syndics' Library found their home there by way of David's stall.

The publishers thank Sir William Nicholson for allowing them to reproduce part of his drawing of David at his stall; and the editors of *The Times*, *The Spectator*, *The Cambridge Review* and *The Cam* for permission to make this reprint. Any profits from the sale of the book will be handed to Mrs David.

CONTENTS

Frontispiece   By Sir William Nicholson

Appreciations: PAGE

    I By T. R. Glover   9

   II By Sir Arthur Quiller-Couch   15

 III By W. H. D. Rouse   19

 IV By H. F. Stewart   22

  V By S. C. Roberts   28

The Song of David   33

The portrait facing " The Song of David " is reproduced from a pen drawing by Hubert David.

I

SEVENTY and more years ago a boy was born in France who was destined to play a large part in the life of English Cambridge, and who died on Friday.* He was not a man of science, and only in a limited sense a man of letters; he wrote nothing; he held no chair in the University and he had no degree; but few men in the last generation have influenced Cambridge men more deeply, stirred more men to the pursuit of knowledge, or given so much honest pleasure to hundreds of those who think and teach. He kept a bookstall on the Market Place.

In the nineties he appeared in Cambridge; it was a stroke of genius to set up that bookstall in the market place, and he soon saw that he was right. There he was daily to be seen—but not on Thursdays. Thursday is the early closing day in Cambridge, so on Thursday as a rule, and at times on other days, David went to the book auctions in London. Anyone who has mingled at all with the Antiquarian Booksellers' Society knows what a figure the old man was among them—at book sales and at their

9

* November 20th, 1936.

annual dinners; they all knew him, and the feeling was kindly. David's forte was not tidiness in shop or garb; he had not the trim personality of Cambridge's other great bookseller, Nicholson, the "Maps" of the famous engraving. David in a dinner-jacket at the annual dinner was a sight to remember; affection was startled into amused surprise; but it was good to see him.

For many years he was on the brink of ruin—at least he said so—always nervous about the new generation of students, the death or removal of steady old customers, the prevalence of the passion for cars over the love of books, the problem of getting his money from his happy-go-lucky young collectors. But he kept afloat and educated his son (the well-known Hubert); and the bookstall at times maintained two assistants along with them. So somebody must have paid bills now and then.

What legends there are of those assistants and their relations with the old man! His nervous temperament made him blaze with wrath at times, and then—— Then, on one occasion, after "getting the sack" on the spot, and being consigned to the most awful dooms, when the old man's breath failed, came the quiet response: "Have you got a cigarette?" and the guilty wretch was forgiven and kept in service till conscription swept him off to serve his country. Another is reported to have said that he "got the sack" every week for fifteen years, and then began to fear the "guv'nor" was in bad health, when the sixteenth year wore through without the weekly "sack". He tells of his first "sack" when he was a lad, and how he sadly went across the market, pursued by the "guv'nor", with a shilling and instant restoration.

In early days men sought folios, he used to say, and *incunabula*; in late years he added "remainders" to his trade. Probably no bookseller has ever sold so many first editions of Dickens—certainly not in Cambridge; but if you preferred Thackeray, or Borrow, or Trollope, all you had to do was to pay a daily visit, and sooner or later everything collectable came to the stall, and generally at prices that even college people could afford. For he shared his luck with his customers; if he bought cheap they had the advantage of it. He borrowed a system

11

of marking his prices from an old master of his abroad. Some phrase in a foreign tongue gave him letters with numerical meaning, and his books were marked g/l and $m/-$ and $r/-$ and so forth. These letters in a bold, sloping hand must be in thousands of volumes all over England, and every price-mark by now a memento of happy hours at the stall.

Saturday morning was the time—unless you were of the small group of enthusiasts who so sadly hindered him in "marking off" the newly unpacked books on Friday. There was always the chance of a "find". One man boasts an old 1532 Simon Grynaeus bought of David, in which after purchase he found the autograph of Sir Thomas More *ex dono authoris*; another a volume with several lines in the autograph of Martin Luther. One never knew what there might be; there was hardly a field of literature from which something significant might not turn up. As William Bateson, the Mendelist, said, to haunt that stall was a liberal education. So it was; and one wonders how many addicts of bibliography, how many collectors, began there. You bought your first "first edition"; a better copy might appear, and you could exchange with a little profit to David. By and by he came to know your wants—"There's a good *Romany Rye* coming on Saturday"—or *Peter Bell. Don Quixote* in every garb— Shelton, Jarvis, the moderns, and the shameful Phillips—you found them all there sooner or later, with the Spanish and the French; possibly not the Gujerati, but it too may have been there unrecognized. Brown's *Telugu-English Lexicon* turned up on the shilling stall, and was snapped up by a purchaser who had a relative studying Telugu. And the works you got now and then for 6*d*.—Archbishop Benson's *Cyprian*, Sir George Adam Smith's *Isaiah*. A rhymer in the *Cambridge Review* once wrote an address to prospective authors with the refrain "Surely thou shalt come to David!" and it was true. Others came to David. William Nicholson drew him at his stall. Charles Whibley, Lytton Strachey, and "Q.", with a great many more interested in literature, entertained the old man at a luncheon in Trinity; and mighty pleased he was with it, though when he came to reply to the toast of his health words failed him and he sat down quickly and abashed, and rather the more endeared himself by this sincerity.

On Thursday the 19th of November, 1936 he went to London for some book sale. He returned by "the mail" and reached his house at 1.30 a.m. on Friday. About three or so he woke feeling ill, and after a little his wife went to fetch the doctor. When they reached the house David was dead. The end came with merciful quickness. He will be greatly missed. Thirty-eight years of the stall—and how many friends he made! Moody even to grumpiness at times, responsive to a joke, at bottom kindly, constantly helpful—and as for knowledge of books and editions! By a strange chance, on the day of his death the *Review* had a stanza about the booksellers—Deighton, Porter, and the rest—ending:

"And Mr Bowes and Bowes and Bowes,
   He knows—*he* knows—HE knows—HE
      knows!
   And what old David doesn't know
   Is what the telephone calls O—
      Or something even shorter."
                    T. R. GLOVER (in *The Times*)

II

AMONG vanished and fast vanishing features of the Cambridge Market Hill, none will be searched for by habitual eyes and missed with a keener sense of loss than he.

Gustave David was born in 1860 in Paris. Four years later the family—of French descent crossed with Hebrew—moved to Switzerland, where the child received his early education in three languages; thence in the "seventies", under what mysterious direction is not known, migrated to England, to start a book-trade in Gorleston. "At that time", says Boswell, writing in 1709, of Lichfield and of Dr Johnson's father, "booksellers' shops in the provincial towns of England were very rare 'and might only earn with assiduity' a reasonable share of wealth." One may guess that in one hundred and fifty years or more Gorleston had scarcely overtaken Michael Johnson's Lichfield as a literary mart. At any rate another move was made, this time to London; where Gustave, now a grown man, set up in a small business of

15

his own. Whether it wilted, or a narrow street in a Capital palled on him, or (let us believe) urged by the daemon of his genius, one day he put up his shutters, headed for Cambridge and erected a stall; and there for many generations (as generations are counted here) was a centre of his own amid ancient colleges, accepted as belonging to a "University" which, literally translated, means "all of Us".

There it just *was*. And there he stood on all working days save Thursday and Saturday; always smoking but at your service; inscrutable with a subdolent smile which lit up with something like affection on the approach of some tried favourite among his clients. (His greeting of the late Charles Whibley, for instance, had to be witnessed to correct anyone's estimate of his own worth in the scale of David's.) On Saturdays, when the merry costers invaded the market, like some grave Tyrian trader he withdrew to the neighbouring eminence of Peas Hill, and there, among the fried fish stalls, undid his corded bales. Also, if you had hesitated over a purchase or passed in too great a hurry to snap it up, the odds

were you would miss it for ever. It had
been swept back overnight into his shop,
in which to recover it was to search for a
needle in a haystack. Legend even held
that he disposed each day's surplus stock
under the *hic jacets* of St Edward's Church-
yard. On Thursdays he attended the book
sales in London. His method of bidding and
buying there must have obeyed some steady
system into which it is no business of ours
to inquire. But his system of pricing and
selling, long tested, could be accepted as an
honest conspiracy of help between dealer
and purchaser. It was based (if I under-
stand it) on the working out in the long run
of a simple, modest and reasonable per-
centage. He must have been wise enough
to know the money's worth of many a
trouvaille, but sacrificed that knowledge to
his noble reputation for probity.

A spice of vanity may have mixed itself
into this, as into most men's high purposes:
but it once led to the defeat of a lower one.
A few years ago some friends and admirers
planned a luncheon in his honour, and would
have decorated the front of the menu card
with a photogravure of David, singular and

17

familiar personification of something in the *genius loci*. Unhappily, getting wind of this, he faced the photographer in a "gent's boater", frock coat, light trousers and white spats. At the subsequent luncheon in the Hall of Trinity his emotion, expressed in manner rather than in words, went straight to the hearts of all the large company gathered.

An obituary notice in *The Cambridge Daily News* tells us that "his great ambition was to retire and collect old books". This to many will suggest a possible parallel with Omar Khayyam's wonder:

> "What the Vintners buy
> One half so precious as the stuff they sell."

May the stall he founded, and so curiously made his own and the University's, long stand on Market Hill!

"Q." (in *The Cambridge Review*)

III

It is forty years since I first saw David's stall in the Market Place; and ever since then he has been a part of Cambridge to me, as inseparable from the place as King's College Chapel. He knew books well, and he loved a good book well; and some of the finest and rarest of books have been on his stall. I remember the *Nuremberg Chronicle*, and what a fool I was not to buy it! Hakluyt in the first edition, Philemon Holland again and again, Ben Jonson's autographs—but it is too long a story to tell them all. What did strike me as notable was, that David thought of his customers as his friends. He was content with a modest gain upon what he spent, and if he got a good bargain, he was pleased that some customer should do the same. This was just a matter of course with him; but it has made him the friend of all who have dealt with him. He offered me one day a quarto *Dial of Princes*; "you can have it for ten shillings", he said, "it is all scribbled over". So it was; but I found on examining it the signature of Sir Thomas

North at the end, and all the corrections were in his handwriting. When I told David he was simply delighted. He generally spotted a name himself, but he never added to the price on that account. That book is now in the University Library, together with a *Cyropedia* of Philemon Holland containing his autograph—I believe the only known autograph of Holland.

David was never happy except among these old books of value. He cared nothing for fads and fleeting fashions, and he despised the tawdry modern stuff which he had to sell of late years. But there was never anything tawdry about what he chose to buy, unless it came by accident in a job lot. His sixpenny and shilling stores, which came partly from such purchases, were full of interesting books, such as you never see for sale elsewhere. I have bought hundreds of books from him, and I have learnt much from what I did not buy.

I am deeply grateful to him for what he has taught me, and for what he has sold to me; but that would be little without the goodwill and sympathy which went with the sales. David was true gold all through, and he has left a reputation to be envied. We who knew him will never forget him, and we offer our sympathy to his son, a chip of the old block, who has his father's character and tastes. Time will give him his father's knowledge, and I hope he may be like his father the friend of Cambridge men all over the world.

W. H. D. ROUSE (in *The Cam*)

IV

IT is no exaggeration to say that the world of letters is poorer by the loss of David, the Cambridge bookseller, who died at the age of 76 in the small hours of Friday the 20th of November. Ever since he set up his trestles in the Market Place some forty years ago he had been a principal channel through which good literature found its way into the hearts and hands of successive generations of readers, old and young; and his modest stall opened the door for many into the dangerous and delicious garden of Bibliophilia.

When the lamp of learning burnt lowest, during the dreadful years 1914–1918, David, as much as anyone, kept the tiny flame from extinction in Cambridge, tempting cadets and temporary officers with the wares there were no gownsmen to buy; and those who knew this determined, when the University filled up again, to find some means of recognizing his services. A degree *honoris causa* would not have been inappropriate, but precedent and practice forbidding this, his friends gave him a gala luncheon in the hall of Trinity, under the presidency of Mr Arthur Gray, Master of Jesus, the college of Charles Whibley and "Q.", both of whom took active part in the business. David, smartly dressed for the occasion, complete with spats, could not find words to express his feelings, but he was immensely pleased with the compliment thus paid to him. The windows of his shop were long plastered with autograph letters from persons of distinction who wished him well but were prevented from attending his Prytaneum.

Gustave David was a Frenchman and Parisian by birth, *un enfant de la balle*, son of a second-hand bookseller; and it was a pleasure to hear him talk French to a passing compatriot. He brought into Cambridge a flavour of the *Quais*. Like the owners of the boxes which tempt and disappoint the stroller along the Seine, David had a store from which he drew his stuff, besides the weekly consignment of treasures and rubbish gleaned from London sales. This store was for many years housed in a couple of cottages, chock-a-block with books, down in Barnwell. Later on he either sold the cottages as they stood or transferred their contents to a shop in Green Street, whence he presently migrated to St Edward's Passage, off the King's Parade. When the building of the Arts Theatre and the new King's Hostel demolished all around, David's shop, like the house of Pindarus, was partly spared, and there, or in an adjacent house, the business will, we hope, be carried on, perhaps with smaller stock, by his devoted son.

The stock of David *père* was vast and chaotic—an occasional MS., in better days some *incunabula*, "association" books, Elzevirs, masses of seventeenth- and eighteenth-century literature, jostled first editions of Thackeray, Dickens, Scott, Galt, and all the volumes without which no gentleman's and no student's library is complete. From time to time, at rare intervals, a catalogue was issued, but David probably never knew what he had and what he had not, so that shop and stall formed a happy hunting-ground for the book-lover. He didn't know, and did not greatly care; he was no expert, no Quaritch nor "Maps", though he provided the means by which experts are made. What he really cared for was his clients whose individual taste he cultivated and fostered, sometimes setting aside for possible future purchase by Mr X, even at a sacrifice, a book which Mr Y was ready to purchase on the nail. It would be an insult to his memory merely to say that he was an honest bookseller. The charm about him was that you could always be sure that the price at which he offered you a volume was only a slight advance upon what he had paid for it at the sale. If he had had it at a bargain, so had you. This policy brought its reward. Customers came again and again, breaking off their walk to and from work to see what David had on his stall.

A single instance will serve as illustration. A reverend canonist picked up from him a copy of Lyndwood's *Provinciale* for, say, 2*s*. 6*d*. As he pocketed it he remarked, "I never knew Lyndwood fetch less than 30*s*." David, being commiserated on the difference between *esse* and *posse*, said with a snigger "It does me no harm, and it pleases him; he'll soon come back sniffing around for another bargain." He had a fine and valuable moral sense. He held no traffic with what the trade sometimes enters in catalogues as "facetiae", or "curious", such as might do harm to youth and offend the guardians of youth. He wanted no one's morals to suffer from what he supplied.

He died in harness, *felix opportunitate mortis*. His weekly custom was to visit London on Thursday (early closing day at Cambridge) for sales or other business, returning thence by the midnight train. It was just after such an expedition that he had a heart attack, and passed away before a doctor could attend him.

Cambridge will miss the old fellow as he sat in all weathers at his post, reading a story-book from his own stall, smoking endless cigarettes, and mildly grumbling at the degeneracy of the age ("Under-graduates don't buy as they did in Mr Keynes's time"), at the high prices of the market, at the difficulty of making both ends meet. When the fever of collecting had cooled or when crowded shelves forbade further acquisitions, David was gently reproachful, "We don't see you often now"; but he understood and he never failed of loyalty and affection towards an old client.

The annals of book-collecting are full of romance and David deserves a niche in the Temple beside Thierry and Pancoucke, Andrew Millar, the Dillys and the adorable antiquaries of Anatole France. He might well have adopted and adapted the advertisement of William Caxton. "If any man wants a good book, let him come to me in the Cambridge Market Place, and he shall have it good cheap."

H. F. Stewart (in *The Spectator*)

V

I TAKE as my text a sentence of Mr Glover's:
"Some phrase in a foreign tongue gave him
[David] letters with numerical meaning,
and his books were marked *g/l* and *m/-* and
r/- and so forth. These letters in a bold,
sloping hand must be in thousands of
volumes all over England."

This, surely, is David's greatest memorial.
Every client of his can wander round his
shelves and point to a number of volumes
snapped up at some ridiculously low figure.
Sometimes, it is true, the condition is not
very good, but even if you bought a book
in poor condition, the same book would,
sooner or later, turn up on the stall in a come-
lier form and you were free to return your
inferior copy, with a few shillings thrown
in, in exchange for the finer specimen.

Once I bought a set of Horace Walpole's
Works (five volumes, quarto, 1798). It was
a clean copy, but was cased in an abominable
binder's cloth of the later nineteenth cen-
tury. Some years later the same work
appeared on the stall in contemporary calf

and in very good state. The exchange was easily and cheaply effected. Inside each volume of the calf-bound set were the book-plate and shelf-mark of Richard Brinsley Sheridan. I don't think David had noticed this additional feature; but he was delighted when I pointed it out to him.

As an undergraduate, I had not properly known David. I had bought one or two books, simply because they were cheap; but I had not really known what I wanted. But as soon as David knew the kind of book you were looking for, your relationship with him became easy. "I put something aside for you yesterday", he would say.... "Hubert/Charley, what was that book I said Mr Roberts would be sure to buy?" Out it came—a Trollope (rather shabby, probably, but Trollope "firsts" in "fine" condition were beyond me); or a book on old Cambridge; or a novel of the nineties; or some satisfying eighteenth-century quarto in calf or even in paper boards.

It was a safe policy to buy anything in original boards at David's. Years ago, before I understood its value, I bought such a copy of Mrs Piozzi's *Anecdotes of Doctor Johnson*.

Later, I realized that it was the first of the four editions published in 1786. It was entirely uncut and altogether in first-rate condition —the price was one shilling. For the same price I secured the first edition of Warton's *Essay on the Writings and Genius of Pope* (1766).

One of the charms of David's stall was that you never knew what you might find inside the cover; there was no labelling of "association copies"; if you found something interesting on the title-page, it was your lucky day—and that was all. Thus I have a copy of Warton, *History of English Poetry* (three volumes, quarto, 1774) which is inscribed as a presentation copy from the author to W. Lloyd. Again, I find on my shelves a copy of the second edition of Horne Tooke's *Diversions of Purley* (two volumes, quarto, 1798). It is not a very exciting work, perhaps, but this copy contains a letter written by Horne Tooke from Wimbledon to Mr Thomas Hardy, Shoemaker, Fleet Street, congratulating him on the defeat of the hellish plot against him. For the two volumes I paid, apparently, three or four shillings.

Rather more expensive were a first edition of *Emma* (lacking half-titles, alas) and the eleven volumes of the first edition of Pope's *Homer*, well preserved in a contemporary binding. But, in fact, how cheap they were and how well they look. And then the oddments, the books bought simply because they were irresistible at the price of a shilling or so—Pickering's reprint (with its lovely title-page) of Fuller's *Holy State* (1840); the six volumes of Beloe's *Anecdotes of Literature and Scarce Books* (1807–1812) in beautifully clean paper boards; Goldsmith's *Miscellaneous Works* in four volumes; Warren's *Ten Thousand a Year*, a *Yellow Book*, ...

For the most part, one thought of David in association with his stall. But occasionally one saw him in a different *milieu*. Some years ago he was one of the guests at a Coleridge dinner at Jesus College. We dined well and the speeches were lengthy. David, to the embarrassment and the envy of some of his neighbours, frankly went to sleep, his cigar pendent, but firm, in the corner of his mouth. The speech came to an end and the company rose to its feet to drink a toast.

The general movement roused David; he rose with the rest and drained his glass—without removing his cigar. The next time I visited the stall I asked David how he enjoyed the dinner. He looked a little guilty and enquired: "I didn't go to sleep, did I?" I replied that some of us thought he was a little drowsy. "Well," he said, "I'd had a busy day."

May the busy days at the stall go on.

S. C. ROBERTS

THE SONG OF DAVID

AN AFFECTIONATE ADDRESS
TO EVERY INTENDING AUTHOR
INDICATING THE END OF
ALL LITERATURE

THE SONG OF DAVID

Child of Wit, endeavouring
Book to write or song to sing,
   Whether fame by thee be cravèd,
Whether pride or pity stir,
Or mixed hopes thy vision blur,
   Hast thou never thought of David?

Deep in dark St Edward's Lane
Lie the heaps of authors slain—
   Dost thou think thou shalt be savèd?
Scarce a decade may have past
Ere thy volume shall be cast
   In the charnel-house of David.

Though thy style be fine or crude,
Though thy tale be of the lewd
   Or the chaste and well-behavèd,
Be thy works of purest Science,
Place thereon no vain reliance—
   Surely thou shalt come to David.

Racing Calendar, or tome
Steeped in lore of Greece and Rome,
   Plea for dusky race enslavèd,
Newest new theology,
Dimmest old antiquity—
   Thou shalt surely come to David.

Dost thou dream thou canst assuage
Destiny with pictured page,
  Coloured print or cut engravèd;
Nay, remaindered, foxed and torn,
Sold at auction and outworn,
  Thou shalt surely come to David.

Every work of human brain
Comes at last to Edward's Lane,
  Think not thine can e'er be savèd;
Nay, thou too shalt yet be thrust
Deep in darkness, damp and dust,
  In the sombre house of David.

Cambridge Review, February 1913

Lightning Source UK Ltd.
Milton Keynes UK
UKOW06f1520220315

248279UK00009B/201/P